Dear Math-Minded Families,

Thank you and congratulations for taking your first step towards investing in math mastery for your child(ren). For many, abacus-based math instruction is a new way of doing math. With that in mind, I have designed a very fun and user-friendly system for young children. Be sure that you have your jr.counter (www.mathjr.org) and consider joining our Abacus Math Club (www.mathjr.org).

The Mathematician, Jr. system includes:

- An introduction to the abacus using a simplified abacus called the jr.counter (by sure to purchase yours at www.mathjr.org)
- Ample practice for each skill
- Mental Practice
- An emphasis on positive message using adinkra symbols

You will find that using the jr.counter for calculations, and mental practice will significantly develop and improve not only your children's math ability, but will also enhance their understanding of the fundamentals of math language and number relationships. Additionally, your child will be able to conduct mental calculations and will be able to give a better explanation to how he/she has arrived at their answer.

To help your child's commit to increasing math learning, it would be a great idea to add incentives to the contract on the next page and have all 'parties' sign. This contract will help keep your child motivated.

With Much Math Success,

You Abacus Math Club Guide, Dr. Ameerah Anakaona
Founder of Mathematician, Jr.

✦The Mathematician's Contract✦

I, _____ (Mathematician, Jr.) promise to practice each day

so I can become a super smart mathematician. I will work in a place where I can focus. I

will also be sure to focus very hard when it comes to mental math practice math.

_____   _____

Mathematician, Jr.   Date

_____   _____

Parent/ Witness   Date

Mathematician's Parent Contract

After _____ (Mathematician's name) successfully completes

Math Readiness Workbook Level I, I _____ (Parent/

guardian) promise to (write the reward that your child will receive for completing this

book):

_____

_____

_____.

_____   _____

Future Mathematician, Jr.   Date

_____   _____

Parent/ Witness   Date

AFRICA IS A BEAUTIFUL PLACE!

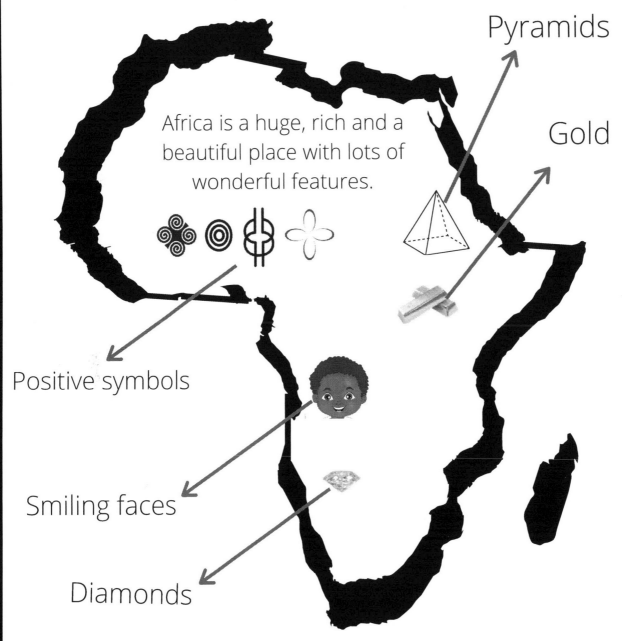

Africa is a huge, rich and a beautiful place with lots of wonderful features.

Positive symbols

Smiling faces

Diamonds

Pyramids

Gold

1

Meet your jr.counter

The jr.counter is a special tool that will help with your math.

Hold your jr.counter up and say: "Hello!"

First lets learn the jr.counter parts!

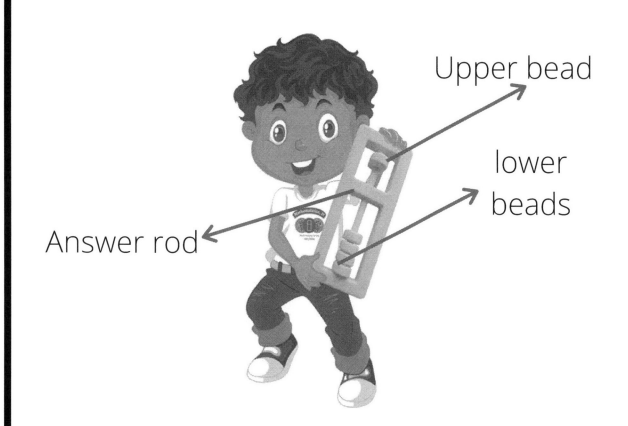

Upper bead

lower beads

Answer rod

www.mathjr.org

Draw a line to match the part name with the correct part
(and practice writing the word)

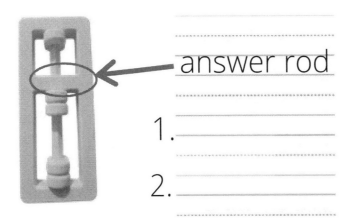

answer rod

1.

2.

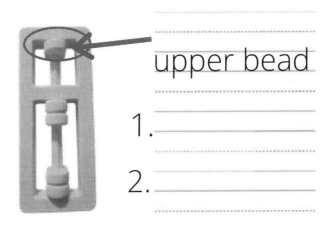

upper bead

1.

2.

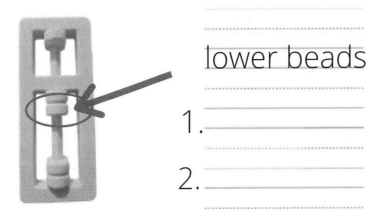

lower beads

1.

2.

Practice writing features of Africa

1. Africa   pyramid   Egypt   gold

2.

1. diamonds   smile

2.

Name one of Africa's features

4

Review your jr.counter's number positions

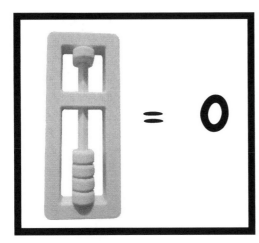 $= 0$

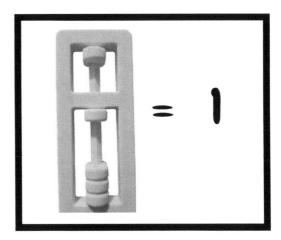 $= 1$

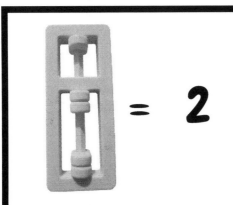 $= 2$

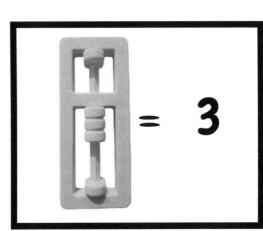 $= 3$

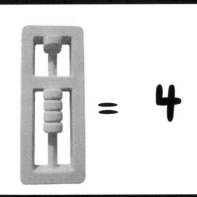 $= 4$

 $= 5$

Review Adinkra Symbols
Created by people of Africa to share positive messages.
Circle your favorite one

| You are a leader | You are very smart |
| You are very strong | You are a hardworker |

Which one are you? Draw it below.

www.mathjr.org

THIS ADINKRA SYMBOL MEANS

YOU ARE A LEADER

Counting 0 - 5
Draw a line to match the symbols in the circle to the correct jr.counter position

you are a leader

Counting Down 0-5

Practice counting down on your jr.counter. Follow the
numbers and move the beads on your jr.counter to follow.
*move beads toward the answer rod

5	4	3	2	1	0

4	3	2	1	0

3	2	1	0

2	1	0

Counting 0-5
Draw a line to match the number to the jr.counter position

 0 5 2 4 1 3

www.mathjr.org

Counting 0-5

Draw a line to match the object number with the jr.counter position

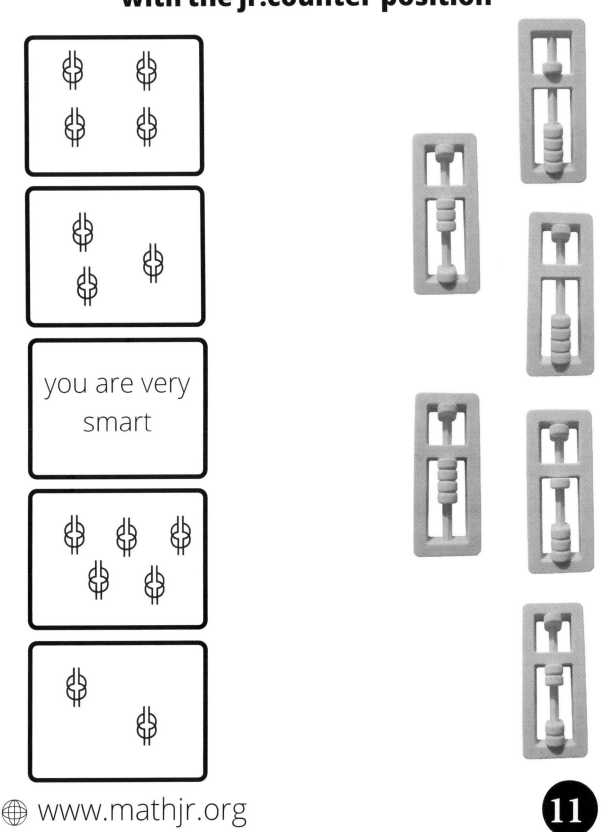

you are very smart

Counting UP 0-5

First, fill in the missing numbers. Then practice
counting up on your jr.counter.
*move beads toward the answer rod

0		2	3		5

0	1		3	4	

	1	2			5

0	1		3		

www.mathjr.org

Counting Down 0-5

First, fill in the missing numbers. Then practice counting DOWN on your jr.counter.

*move beads away from the answer rod

5	4	3		1	

	4		2		0

		3		1	

5					0

 www.mathjr.org

13

YOU ARE VERY STRONG

Counting and Ordering Objects 0-5

Ordering means putting your numbers or objects in order.
See examples of ordering smallest to largest below.

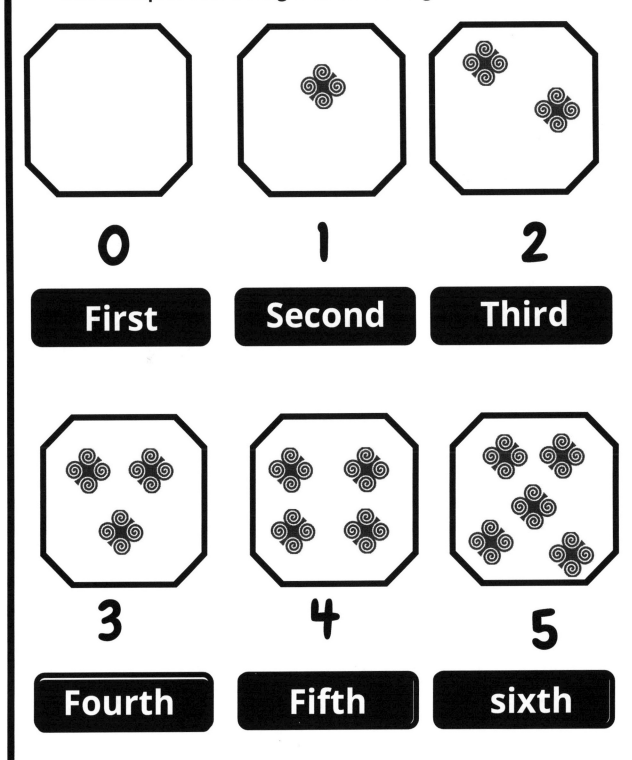

0

1

2

First **Second** **Third**

3

4

5

Fourth **Fifth** **sixth**

Counting and Ordering Objects 0-5
Draw a line to show the order of Adinkra symbols from smallest to largest.

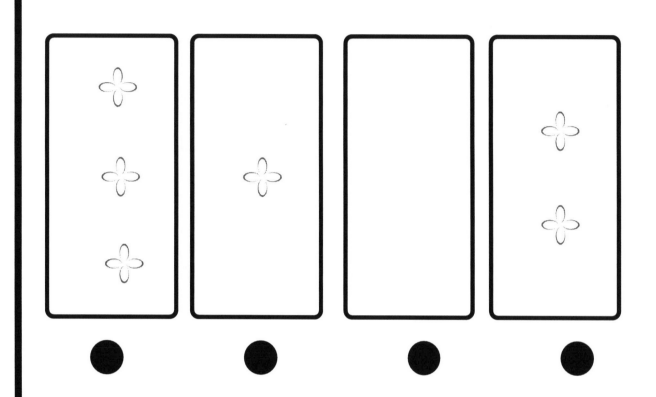

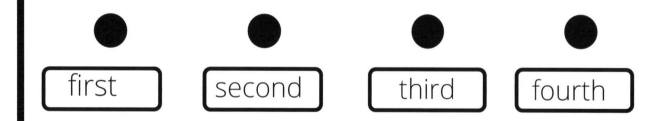

first   second   third   fourth

YOU ARE HARD WORKER

www.mathjr.org

Counting and Ordering Objects 0-5

Draw a line to show the order of jr.counters from smallest to largest.

first	second	third	fourth
●	●	●	●

● ● ● ●

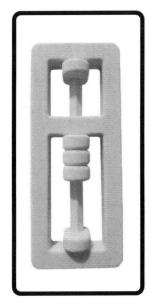 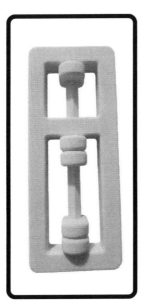 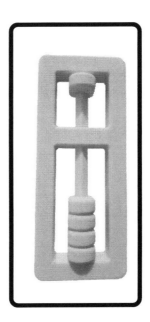 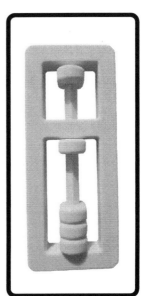

Pyramids

Pyramids are amazing buildings with the shape of a 4-sided triangle that people of Africa called Egyptians built.

Some are as big as castles.

Egyptians were so smart that no one can figure out how they were able to build such amazing buildings.

See how many pyramids you can find in this book?

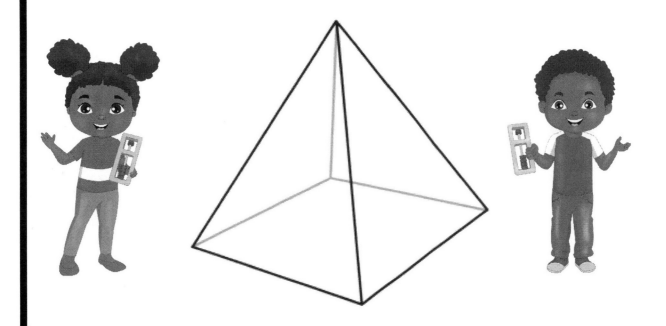

www.mathjr.org

Ordering Objects By Size

Place a check next to the groups of objects that are correctly in order by size smallest to largest.

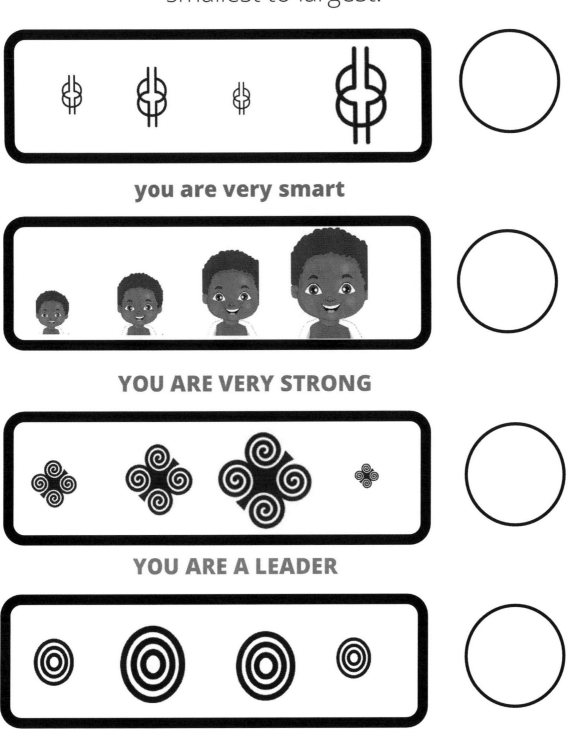

you are very smart

YOU ARE VERY STRONG

YOU ARE A LEADER

Ordering Objects By Size
Place a check next to the groups of objects that are correctly ordered by size smallest to largest.

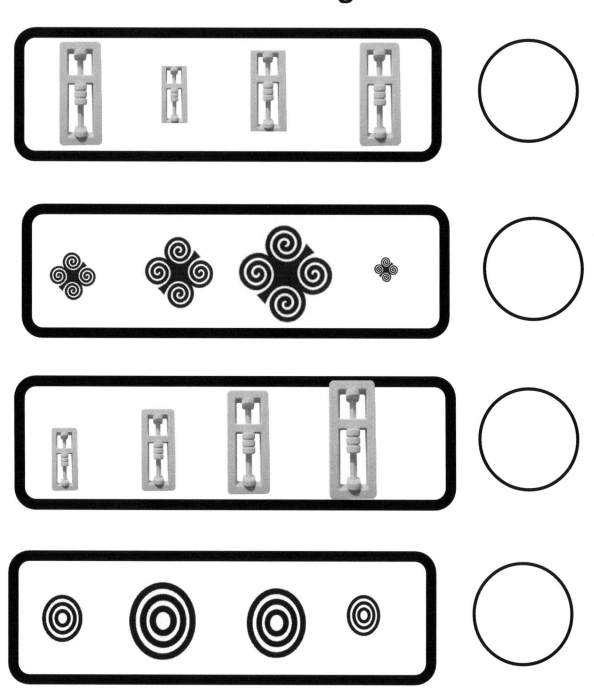

www.mathjr.org

Ordering Objects by Size

First, color Africa. Next, place a check
next to the groups of objects that are correctly in
order by size smallest to largest.

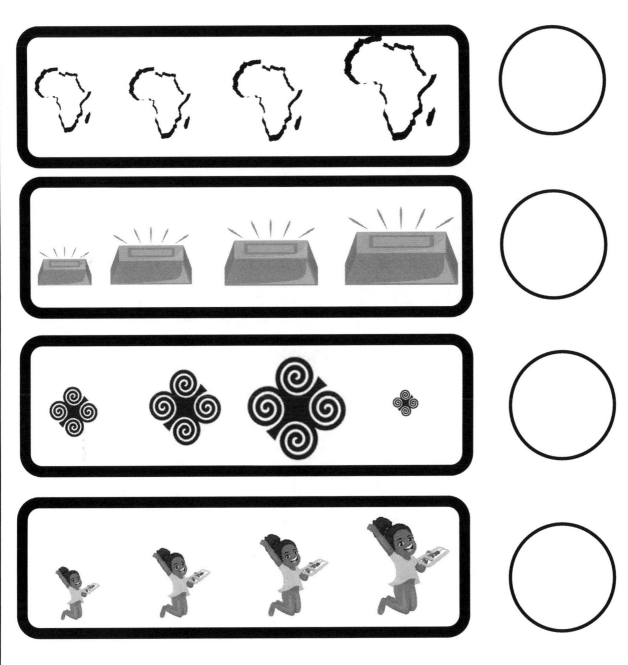

you are very strong

Ordering Objects by Size
Place a check next to the groups of objects that are correctly smallest to largest.

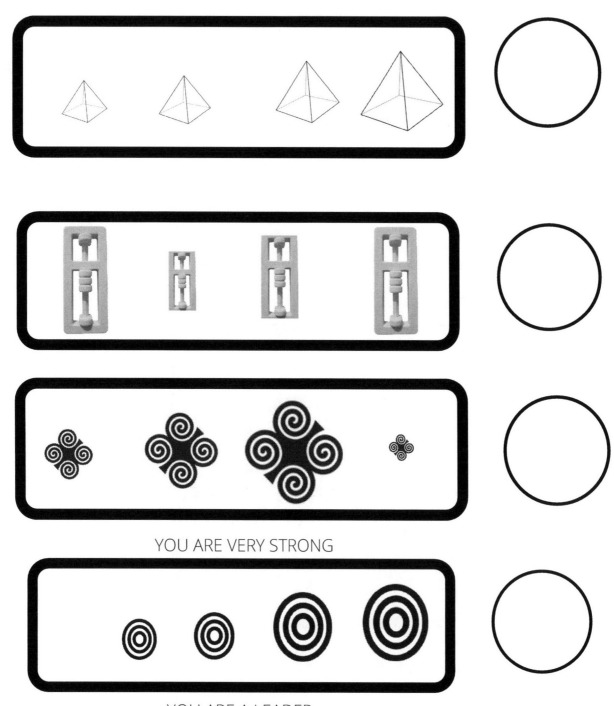

YOU ARE VERY STRONG

YOU ARE A LEADER

Circle the name of the continent below

Asia   Africa   Australia   Antarctica

Circle some of the wonderful features of Africa

diamonds   gold   cold

Pyramids   dolls   smiling faces

23

Ordering Numbers
Re-write the numbers in the correct order

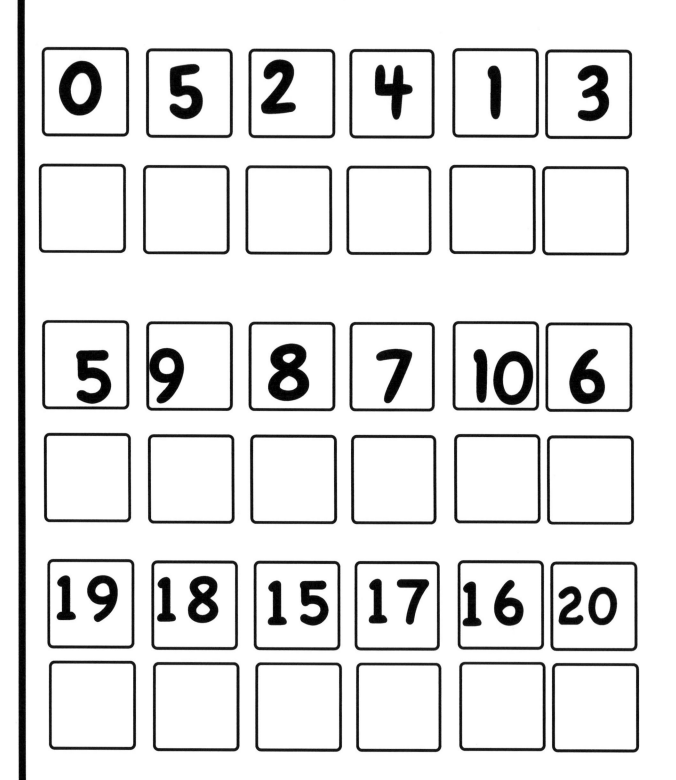

Ordering

Place a check next to the group of jr.counters that are correctly ordered smallest to largest.

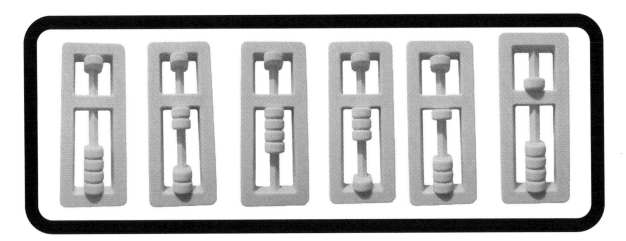

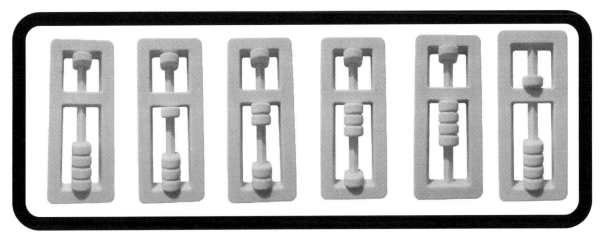

Ordering

Place a check next to the group of jr.counters that are correctly ordered largest to smallest.

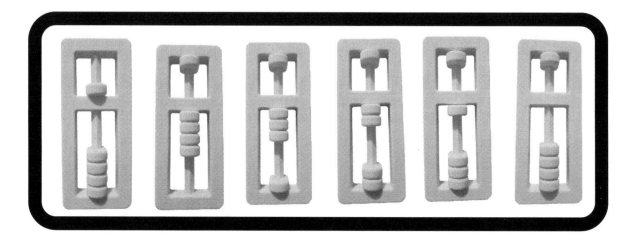

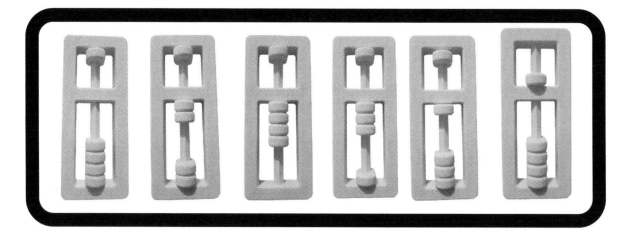

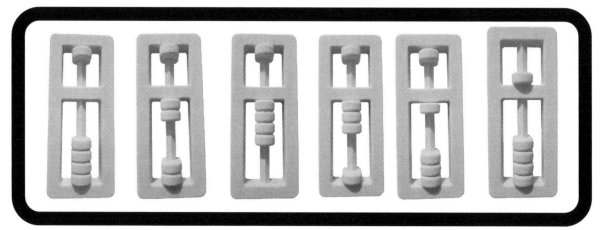

Let's learn to count and position numbers 6-9 on your jr.counter!

Positioning 6-9 on your jr.counter

Positioning 6, 7, 8 and 9 is easy. Look at the positions below and see how they are different from 1, 2, 3 and 4. Circle what is different with 6, 7, 8 and 9.

*Hint: look at the upper bead

6	7	8	9

1	2	3	4

www.mathjr.org

Positioning 6-9 on your jr.counter

Positioning 6, 7, 8 and 9 is easy. See the positions below and practice on your jr.counter.

Start with #5

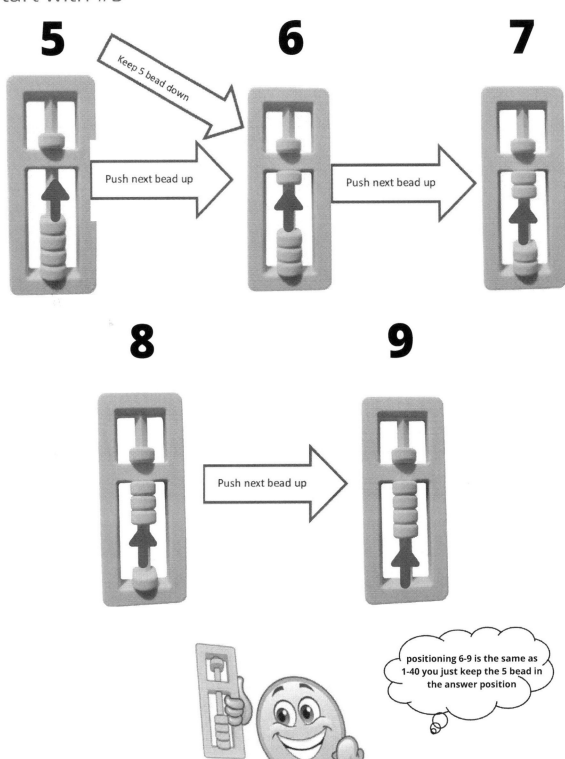

positioning 6-9 is the same as 1-40 you just keep the 5 bead in the answer position

THIS ADINKRA SYMBOL MEANS

YOU ARE VERY SMART

www.mathjr.org

Position 0-9 practice

Write the number the that **jr.counters** are positioned to.

Position 0-9 practice
Write the number that jr.counters are positioned to.

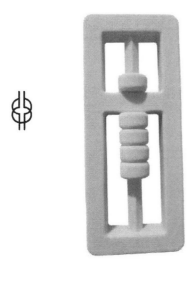

Position 0-9 practice

Write the number the that jr.counters are positioned to.

Position 0-9 practice

Write the number the that jr.counters are positioned to.

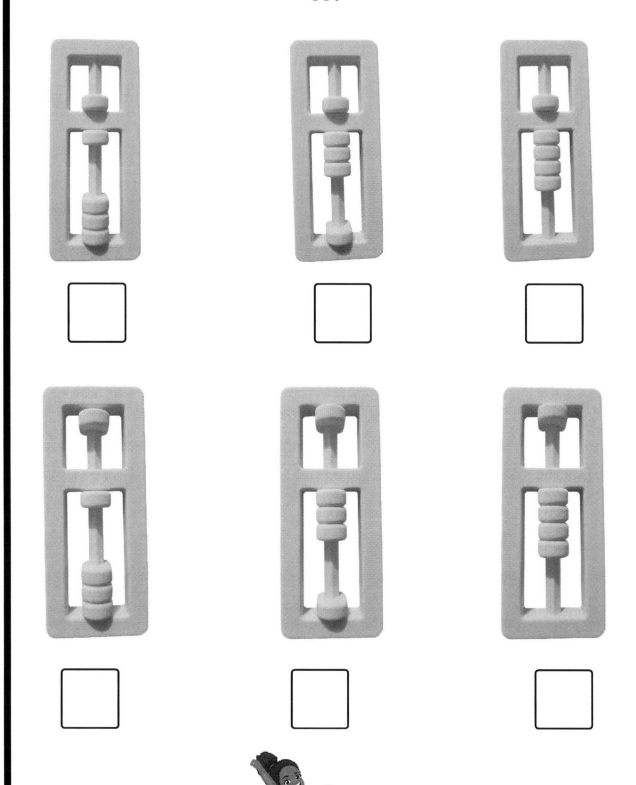

www.mathjr.org

Counting to 9 on your jr.counter

To count to 9 you need to do the "the switcheroo" for 5, than add your lower beads. Its easy! Look below and follow along and practice on your jr.counter.

5   6   7   8   9

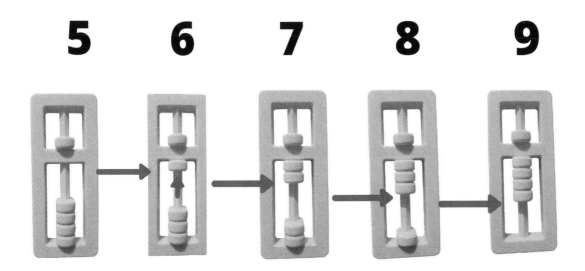

| Start at #5 position | Add first lower bead to count to 6 | Add next lower bead to count to 7 | Add next lower bead to count to 8 | Add next lower bead to count to 9 |

Copy the sentence below and say it loud

 I am very smart

Counting 9 on your jr.counter

Start with the positions below on your jr.counter and practice counting to 9.
Don't forget the "the switcheroo" at # 5.

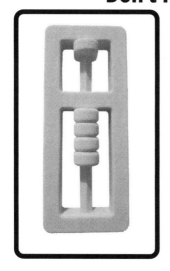 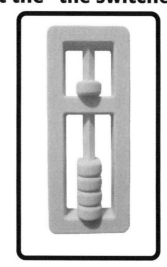 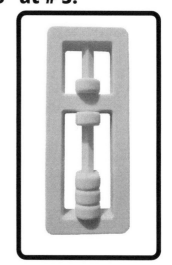

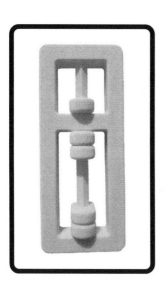 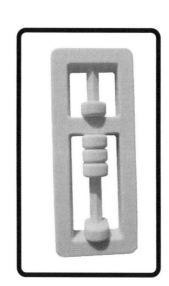 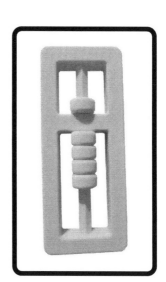

Practice counting
4 to 9 over and
over 10 times

www.mathjr.org

Counting UP 10-30

Fill in the missing numbers.

10	11	12	13	14	15
			19	20	
			25	26	
		30			

Copy the sentence below and say it loud

I am very smart

Counting Down 30-0
First, fill in the missing numbers. Practice counting
DOWN on your jr. counter.
*move your beads away from the answer rod

30					25
24		22			
18			15		
	11				7
			3		
		0			

www.mathjr.org

Thiw Adinkra symbol means...

You are a hard worker

Counting UP 30-50

Fill in the missing numbers.

30	31	32		34	

	37		39	40	

	43		

46		

49	

Let's learn to count
0-5 on your jr.counter!

Counting on the jr.counter is fun!

You get to move beads up and down to make numbers larger and smaller.
Counting is just like bead positioning.

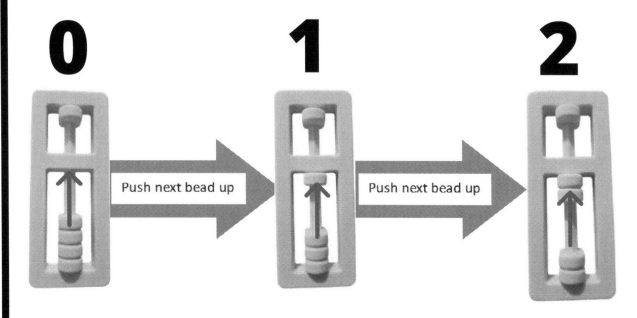

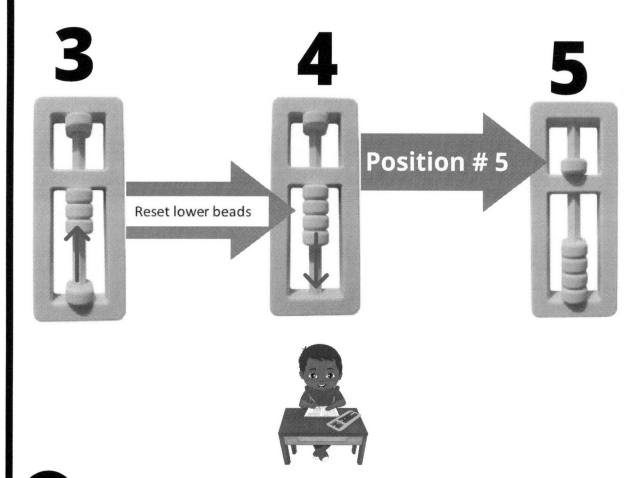

www.mathjr.org

Counting to 5 on your jr.counter
To count to 5 you need to do the "the switcheroo"
To count to 5 you need to do two moves.

Start in the
4 position

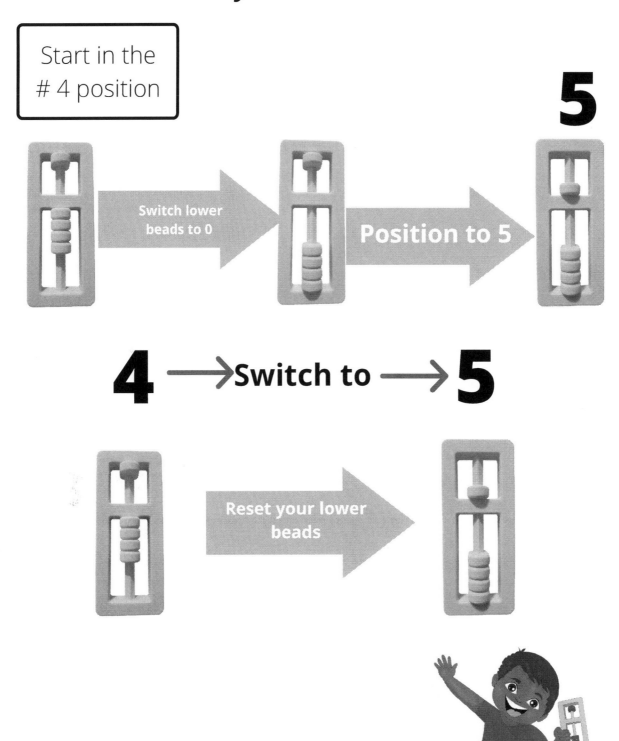

5

Switch lower beads to 0

Position to 5

4 →Switch to→ **5**

Reset your lower beads

Practice the number 5

On your jr.counter practice switching number position called the "switcheroo"

When changing positions from 5 or to 5, you have to do two movements.

from 5 to 1

first move 5 UP to the reset position | Then position your lower beads to the number you want

5 ➡ 1

from 5 to 2

first move 5 UP to the reset position | Then position your lower beads to the number you want

5 ➡ 2

from 5 to 3

first move 5 UP to the reset position | Then position your lower beads to the number you want

5 ➡ 3

from 5 to 4

first move 5 UP to the reset position | Then position your lower beads to the number you want

5 ➡ 4

www.mathjr.org

Let's meet the friends of 5 and 10

Friends of 5
Friends of 5 are our little friends

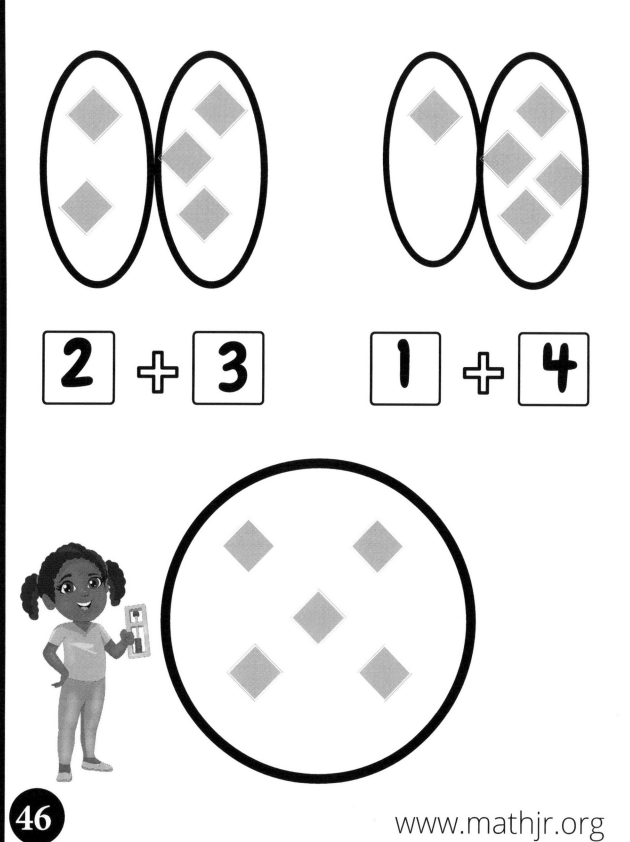

$$\boxed{2} + \boxed{3} \qquad \boxed{1} + \boxed{4}$$

www.mathjr.org

Friends of 5
Friends of 5 are our little friends

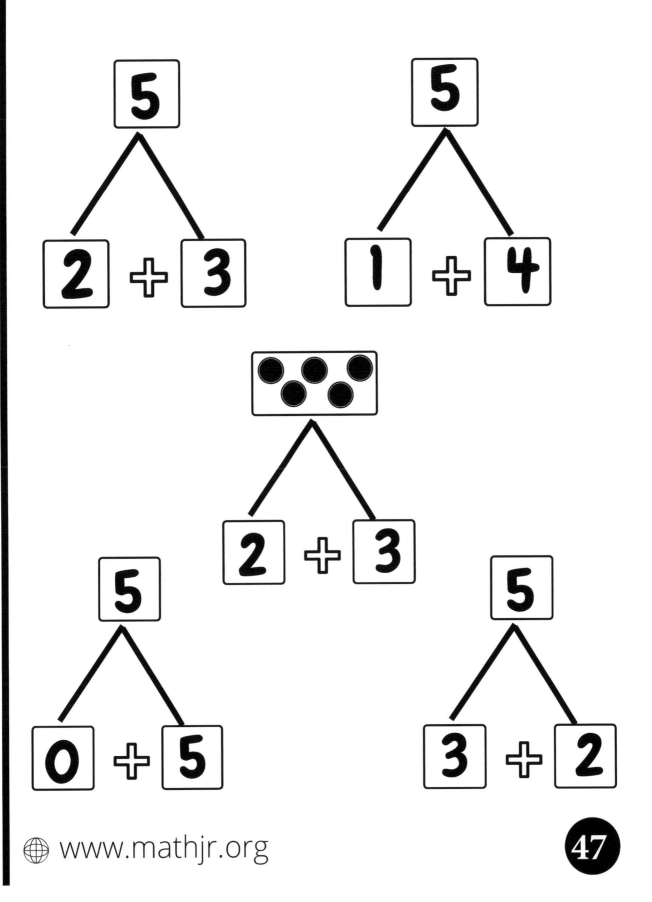

Friends of 5

Complete the addition to make the friends of 5

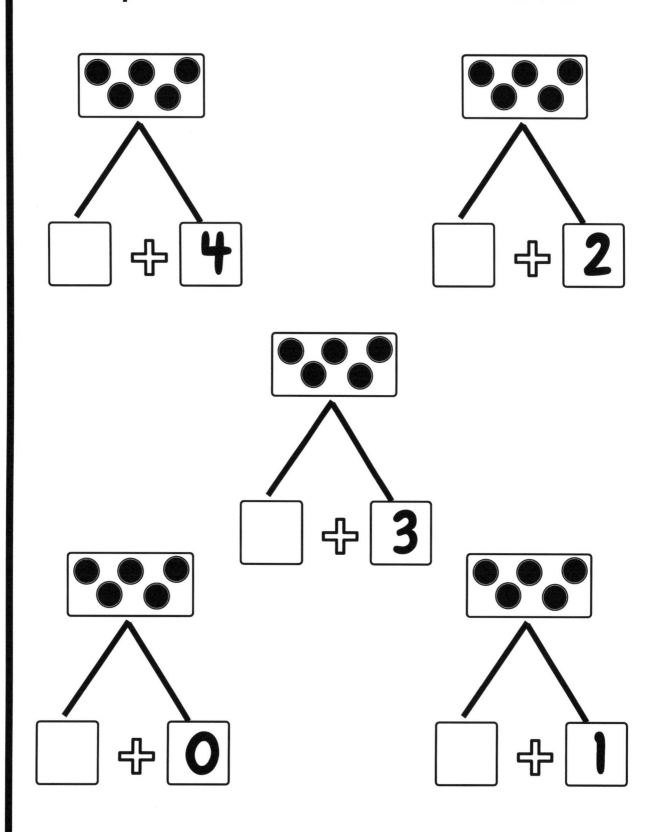

www.mathjr.org

BIG Friends of 10

Friends of 10 are our BIG friends

$0 + 10$ $1 + 9$ $2 + 8$

 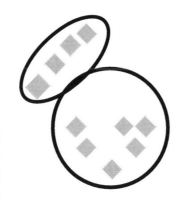 

$3 + 7$ $4 + 6$ $4 + 6$

Friends of 10
Friends of 10 are our big friends

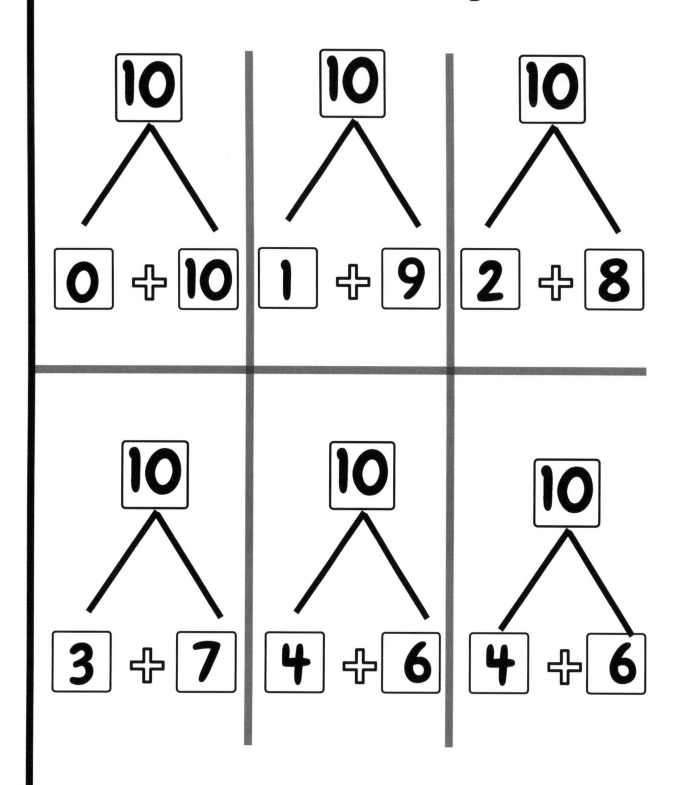

www.mathjr.org

Meet the big friends
Friends of 10

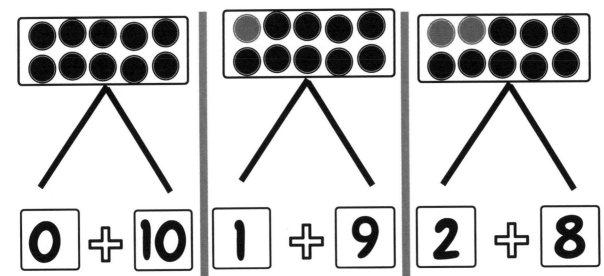

$$0 + 10 \qquad 1 + 9 \qquad 2 + 8$$

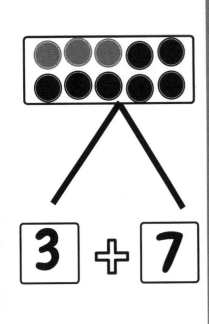 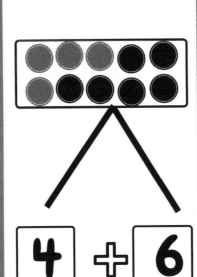 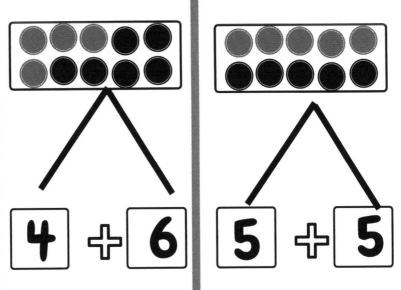

$$3 + 7 \qquad 4 + 6 \qquad 5 + 5$$

Friends of 10
Complete the addition to make the friends of 10

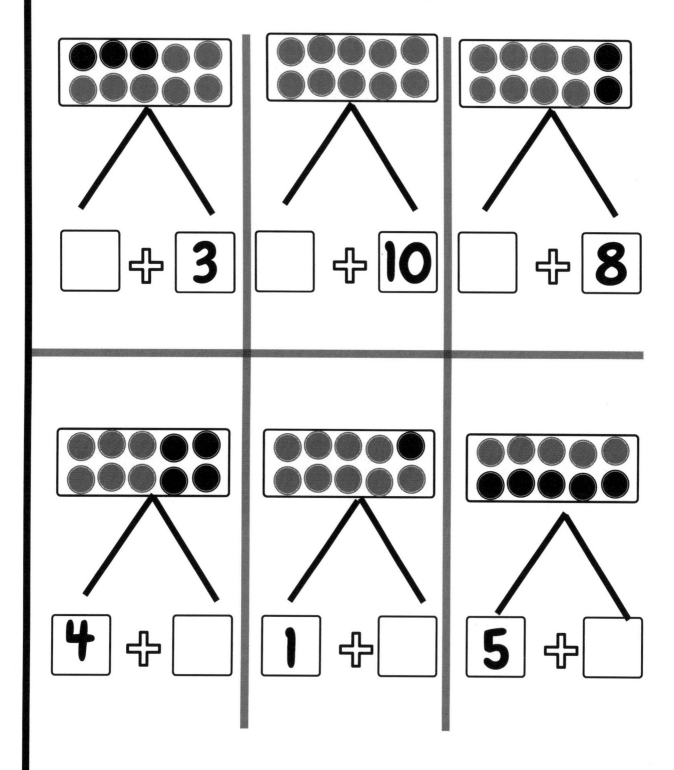

www.mathjr.org

Friends of 10
Complete the addition to make the friends of 10

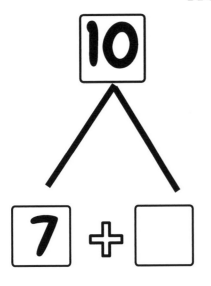

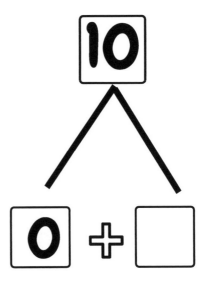

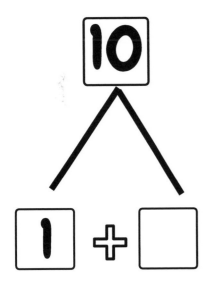

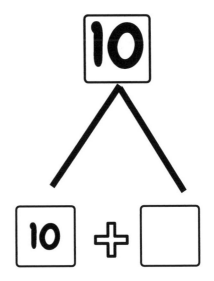

Let's learn to count and position numbers 6-9 on your jr.counter!

Positioning 6-9 on your jr.counter

Positioning 6, 7, 8 and 9 is easy. Look at the positions below and see how they are different from 1, 2, 3 and 4. Circle what is different with 6, 7, 8 and 9.

Hint: look at the upper bead

6

7

8

9

1

2

3

4

Positioning 6-9 on your jr.counter

Positioning 6, 7, 8 and 9 is easy. See the positions below and practice on your jr.counter.

Start with #5

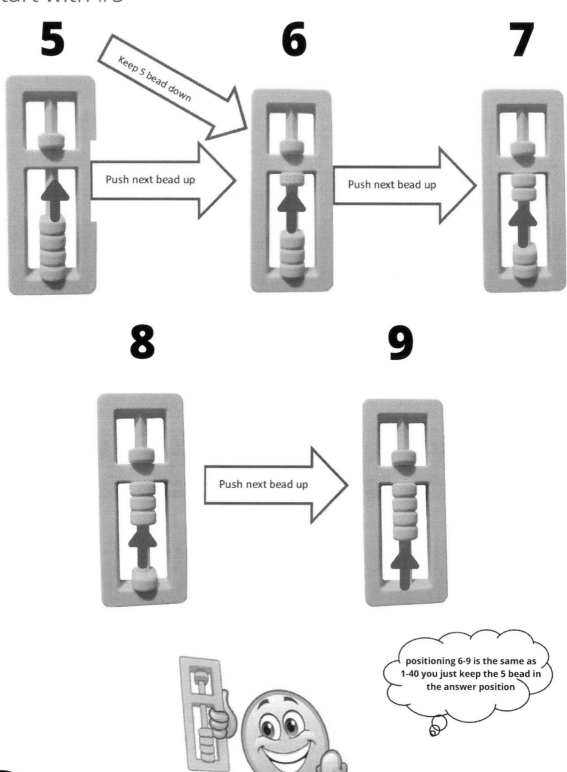

www.mathjr.org

Position 0-9 practice
Write the jr.counter's number.

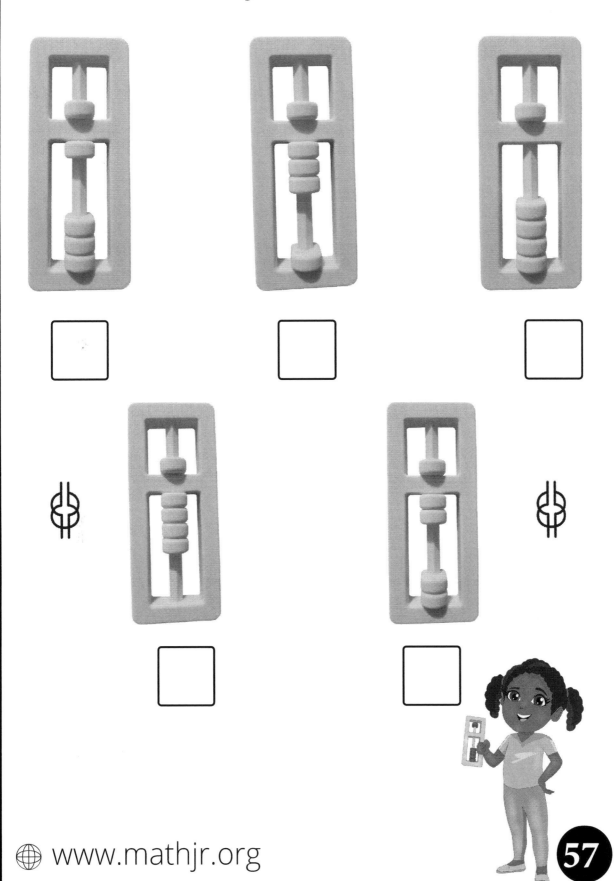

Position 0-9 practice

Write the number the jr.counters are positioned to.

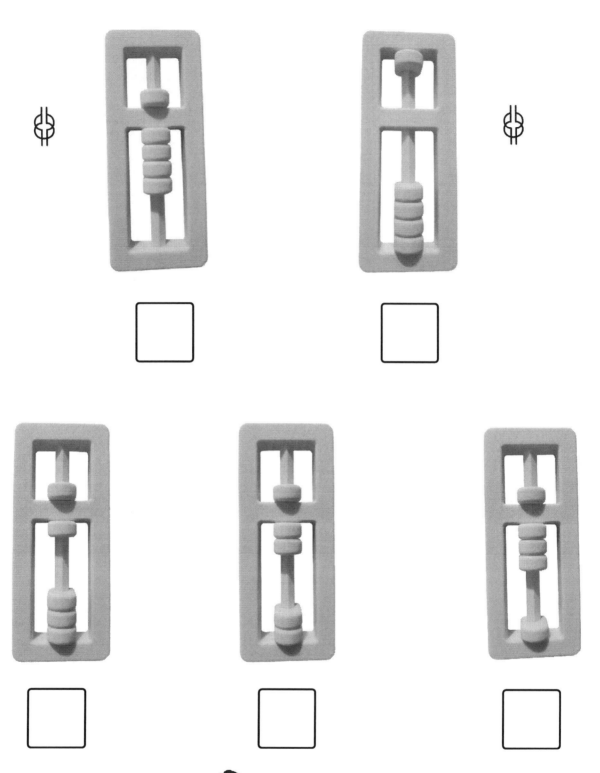

www.mathjr.org

Position 0-9 practice
Write the number the jr.counters are positioned to.

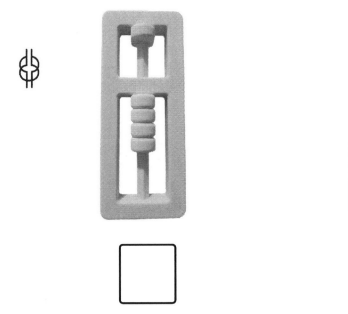

 www.mathjr.org

59

Position 0-9 practice
Write the number the jr.counters are positioned to.

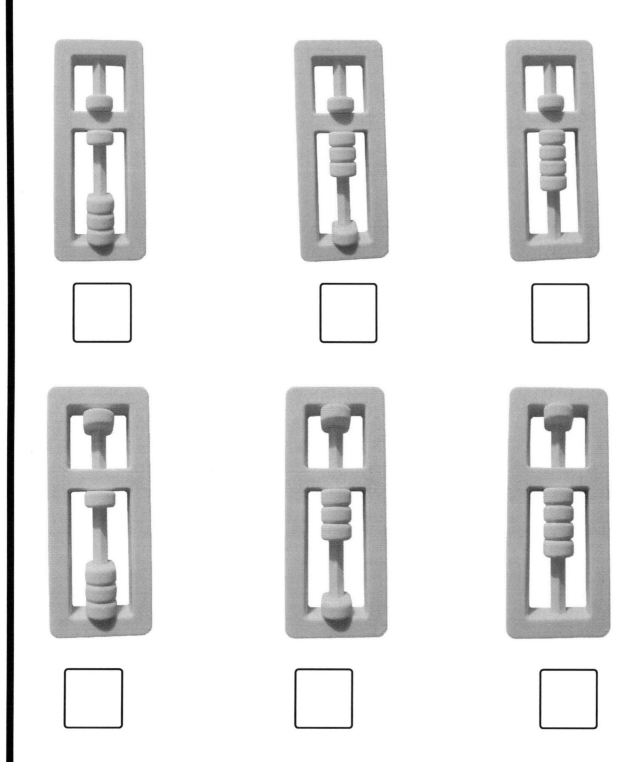

www.mathjr.org

THIS ADINKRA SYMBOL MEANS

YOU ARE VERY SMART

Counting to 9 on your jr.counter

To count to 9 you need to do the "the switcheroo" for 5, than add your lower beads. Its easy! Look below and follow along and practice on your jr.counter.

5　　6　　7　　8　　9

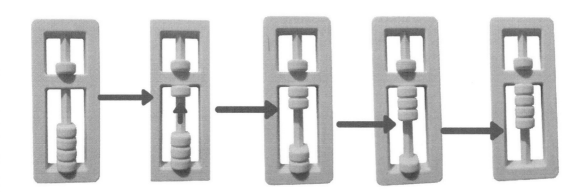

| Start at #5 position | Add first lower bead to count to 6 | Add next lower bead to count to 7 | Add next lower bead to count to 8 | Add next lower bead to count to 9 |

copy the sentence below and say it loud

 I am very smart

Counting 4 to 9 on your jr.counter

Practice counting to 9. Don't forget the "the switcheroo" at # 5.

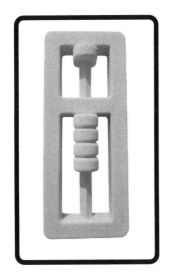
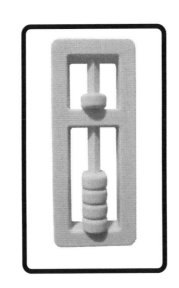
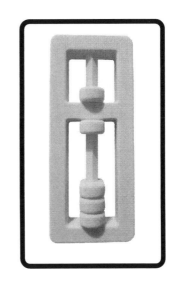

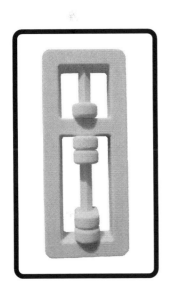
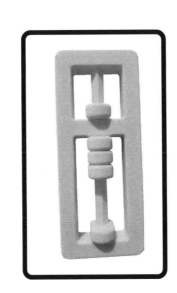
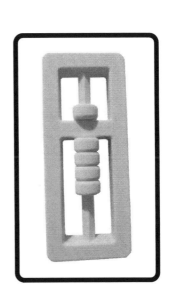

Practice counting 4 to 9 on your jr.counter **10 times**

Counting UP 10-20

First, fill in the missing numbers.

10	11		13	14	15
			19		
				26	
		30			

Copy the sentence below and say it loud

I work hard

Counting Down 20-0

First, fill in the missing numbers.

20	19	18			

14					9

		6

5	4	

		0

Let's learn about number bonds!

Number bonds with numbers 0-4

A bond is something that joins together . Numbers that come together add up to larger numbers.

2 girls + 2 boys = 4 children

2 beads

+

2 beads

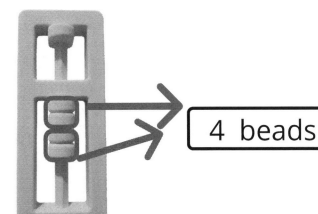

4 beads

THIS ADINKRA SYMBOL MEANS

YOU ARE STRONG

www.mathjr.org

Number bonds

Complete the bonds by writing in the missing numbers.

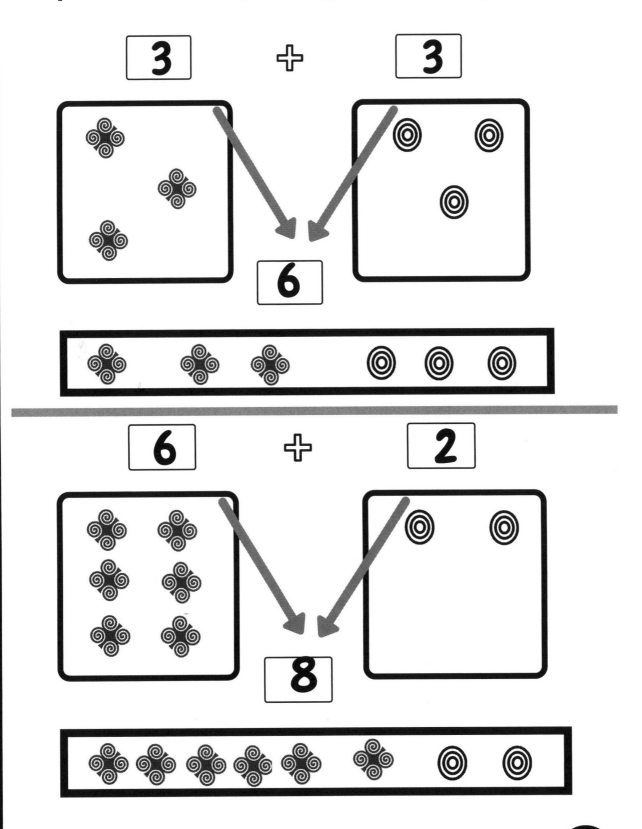

Number bonds

Complete the bonds by writing in the missing numbers.

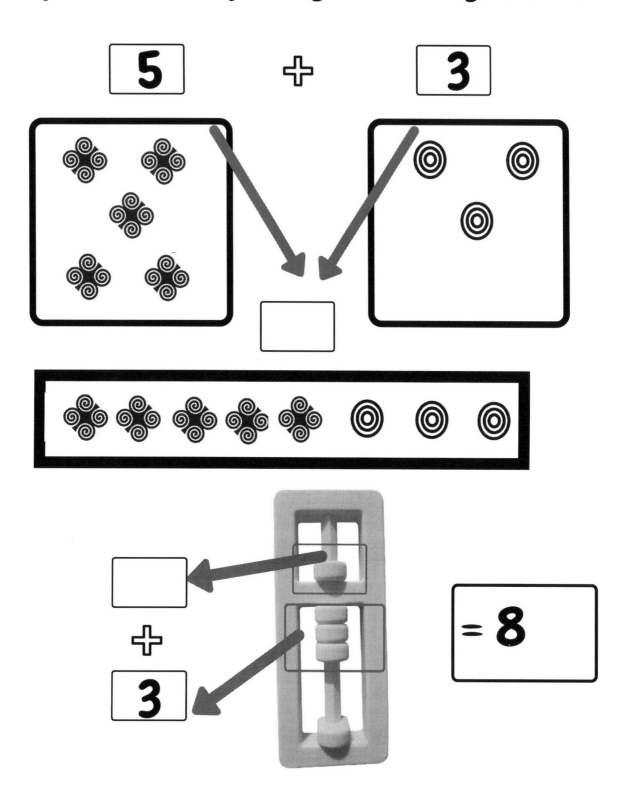

www.mathjr.org

Number bonds

Complete the bonds by writing in the missing numbers.

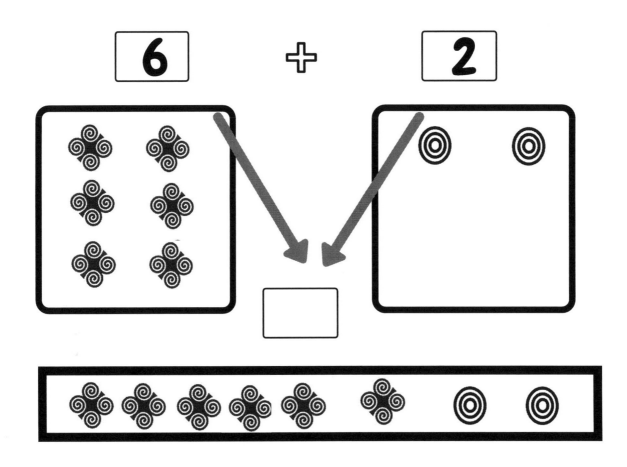

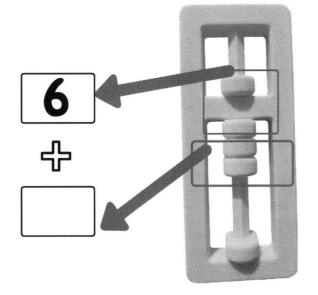

$= 8$

Number bonds

Complete the bonds by writing in the missing numbers.

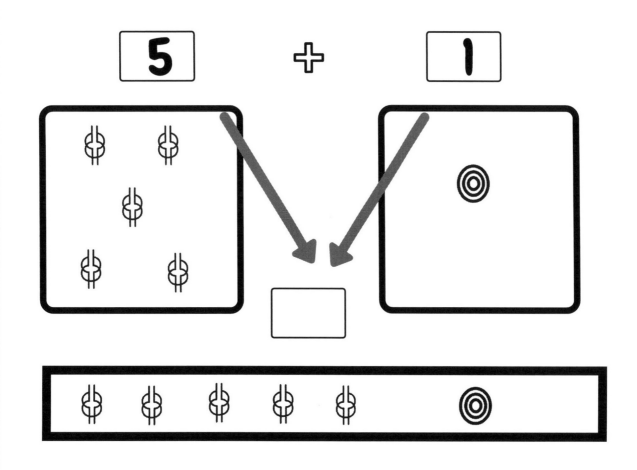

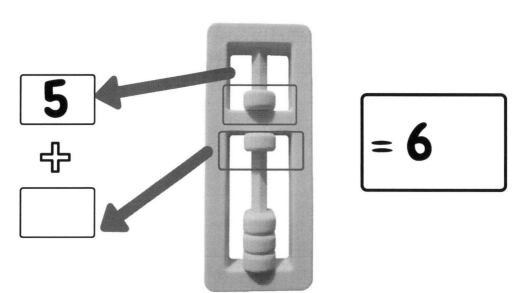

5
+

= 6

www.mathjr.org

Number bonds

Complete the bonds by writing in the missing numbers.

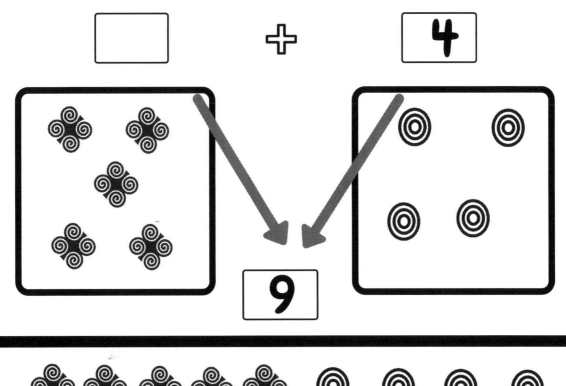

$$\boxed{} \;+\; \boxed{4}$$

$$\boxed{9}$$

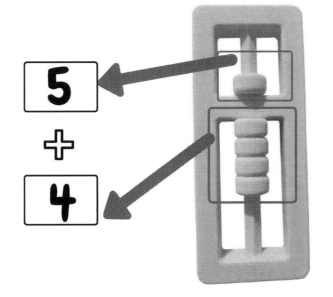

$$\boxed{5}$$
$$+$$
$$\boxed{4}$$

$$\boxed{=}$$

Number bonds

Complete the bonds by writing in the missing numbers.

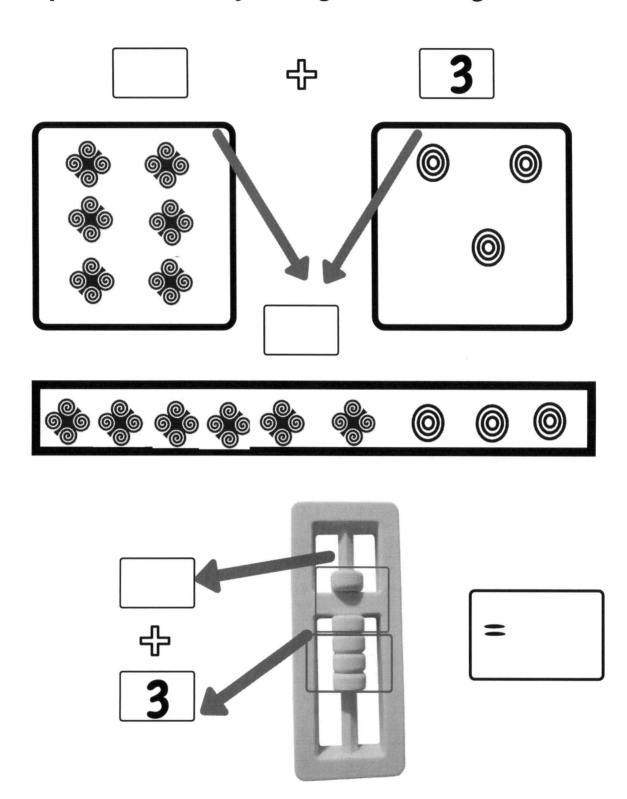

www.mathjr.org

Number bonds

Complete the bonds by writing in the missing numbers.

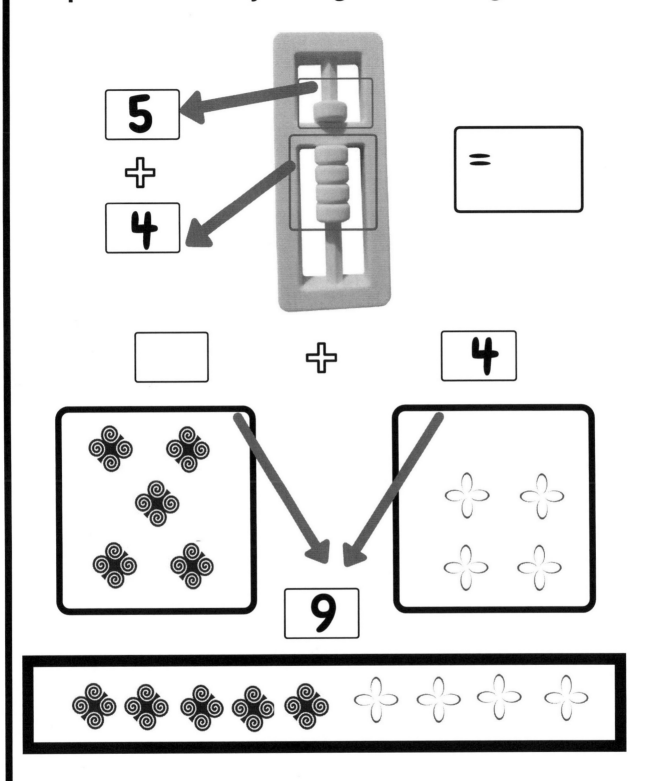

Number bonds

Complete the bonds by writing in the missing numbers.

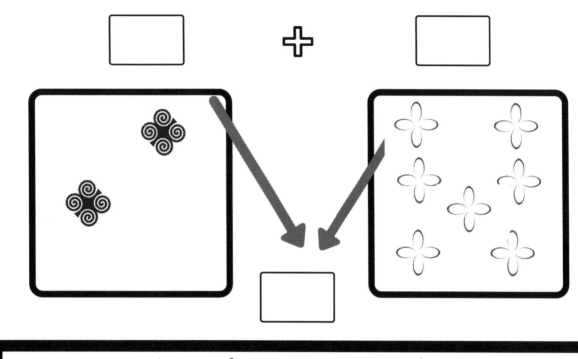

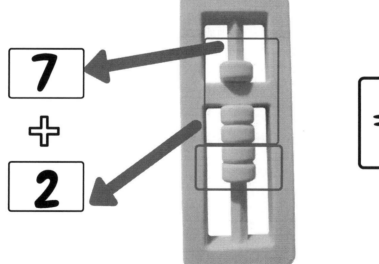

www.mathjr.org

Number bonds

Complete the bonds by writing in the missing numbers.

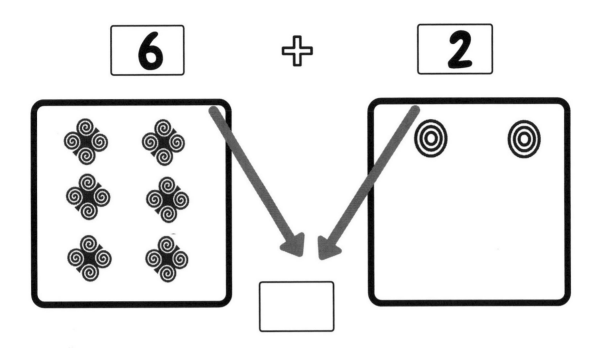

| 6 | ⊹ | 2 |

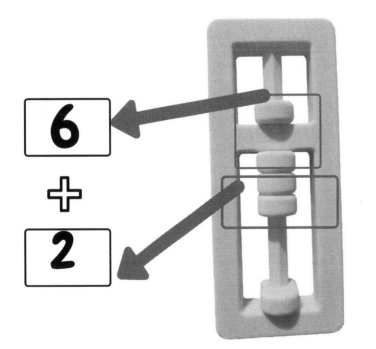

6

⊹

2

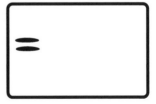

Number bonds

Complete the bonds by writing in the missing numbers.

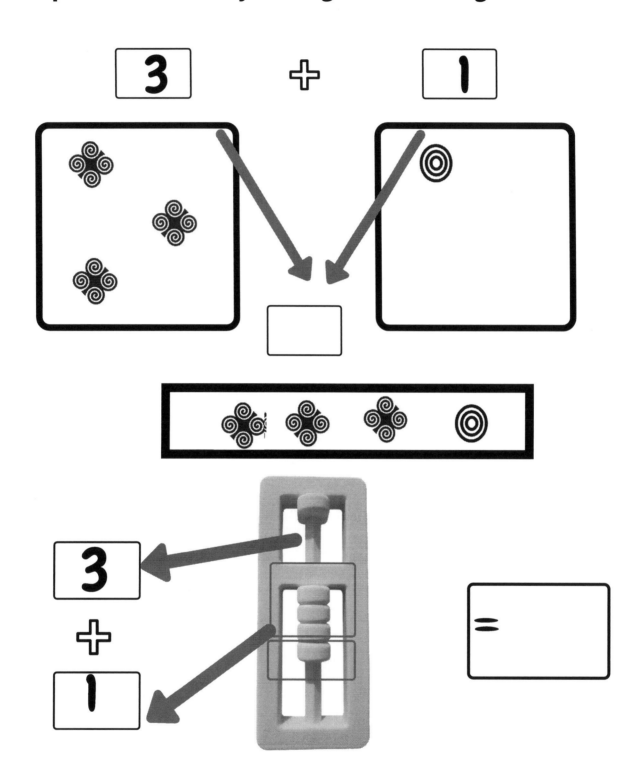

www.mathjr.org

Congratulations!

Your hard work.
Your intelligence.
Your leadership.
Great job completing level 2.
Send us a picture and we will send you
your certificate!
ameerah@mathjr.org

Certificate of Completion

Made in the USA
Monee, IL
15 January 2021